COWGIRL
SADDLE PALS

D1737795

GLADIOLA MONTANA

GIBBS·SMITH
→P
PUBLISHER

SALT LAKE CITY

05   04   03   5   4   3

Copyright © 2000 Gladiola Montana

All rights reserved. No part of this book may
be reproduced by any means whatsoever
without written permission from the publisher.

Published by
Gibbs Smith, Publisher
P.O. Box 667
Layton, Utah 84041

Design by J. Scott Knudsen
Printed in China

Web site: www.gibbs-smith.com
Orders: (800) 748-5439

ISBN 1-58685-001-6

You can't just go
out and get good
saddle pals; they
gotta grow with you.

Everything is
better shared.

When you disagree, try not to be too disagreeable about it.

A promise made is a promise kept.

A saddle pal is the one you turn to when you've just gotta have help.

We pick our friends, we make our enemies, but real estate agents bring us our next-door neighbors.

When you
live for others,
they will live for you.

A crowd is not company. A party is not comfort. A friend is both.

Solitude is the wonder of being alone; loneliness is the misery of being alone.

A good saddle pal remains a good friend, even when you've been rotten.

A good friend will do anything except read the books you insist on lending her.

Of all the good things in this world, a good cowgirl saddle pal is the goodest.

The best way
to keep from
breaking a friendship
is not to drop it.

If at first you
don't succeed,
you'll probably
have more friends.

A true saddle pal will see you through when the rest of 'em see you as through.

Some women have a whole lot of friends; others only have friends they like.

You can't use
your cowgal pals
and have 'em too.

A good saddle pal makes every mile you travel together a little shorter.

If you're too busy
for your friends,
you're too busy.

A friendly ear is the best thing a body can lend.

Saddle pals have a good time doin' somethin' or doin' nothin'. Either way, it's a good time.

Good friends give you love, understanding, and trust; but just as important—they keep your embarrassing little secrets to themselves.

Neither miles
nor days
come between
cowgirl saddle pals.

Friendships should be kept in constant repair lest they get run-down.

Old wood
burns the best.
Old wine tastes the best.
Old books read the best.
Old saddle pals are the best.

No room is
unfriendly
where a friend waits.

Friends have open hearts and minds.

It's the little things that make a big thing out of friendship.

A real saddle pal
walks in when
others walk out.

Sometimes it takes a friend to tell you things you don't wanta tell yourself.

A warm friendship is a comfort no matter what the temperature.

Envy does not belong in a friendship.

Always say "please" when you tell a saddle pal to shut up.

Good saddle pals are good medicine.

When it comes to friends, passing judgment is not a good course to pass.

Friendship is the thread that holds lives together.

Friends grow on you, and the more the better.

When you share your good times with a cowgirl saddle pal, they're even better. When you share your sorrows, they're not as bad.

A loyal
saddle pal
is a strong defense.

L ittle friends
may prove
great friends.

With a
saddle pal,
whatever's fair
is right.

Just because you don't see tears on the outside don't mean it ain't pourin' on the inside.

N
o need to run tests on your saddle pals.

When your horse goes lame, a saddle pal insists that you ride double.

You have a choice in life: saddle pals or loneliness.

There are no
rules for
friendship.

Differences of opinion are the glue of friendship.

If it bothers a saddle pal, it bothers you.

Never miss a
chance to
cheer a friend on.

A good
saddle pal
comes through
like sunshine in
the rain.

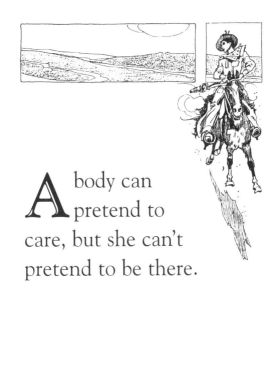

A body can pretend to care, but she can't pretend to be there.

When arguing with a saddle pal, always remember this little phrase: "Maybe you're right."

Lonesome brings on ailments that only company can cure.

Advice is kinda like a fresh pot of chili: You should try a little of it yourself before you start passing it out to your friends.

Share your wisdom, not your prejudices.

There's no need for a lot of talking when two people understand each other.

To bring someone into your life, take a step into hers.

From rocking horse to rocking chair, saddle pals ride together.